Ruth is currently working on her next two books

"The Hexagon of Life – Inspirational Words for Each Day"
and
"Your Journey of Life from Birth to Death – A Book of Self-Discovery"

Just read what others say about
'Musings of a Blogger – Inspirational Thoughts for Your Life's Journey'!

"I just finished reading Ruth Caukwell's new book, *Musings of a Blogger - Inspirational Thoughts for Your Life's Journey*. Let me just say, if you have been struggling in your life, unsure how to identify and break free of the *"baggage"* that's been holding you back, then you have to pick up a copy of Ruth's book. Not only does she help you identify those obstacles, but helps you crush them with a very simple, yet thorough, step by step process. With a format that is easy to use individually, or along with others, this book will become your go-to resource for any struggles you're experiencing in your life.

Rick Sheninger - CEO -
One To One Marketing, Author, and Speaker

"It has been proven that true and lasting success is found within the walls of Self-Belief, Self-Confidence and Self-Love! If you're serious about a successful future then read Ruth's book, *Musings of a Blogger – Inspirational Thoughts for Your Life's Journey,* and experience a Journey inside those walls that will lead you to a deep happiness that few people will ever find." This book is a true *life changer* for sure!

Dr. Robert Minzak - Successful Entrepreneur,
Relationship Marketer and Speaker

Ruth Caukwell's book, *Musings of a Blogger – Inspirational Thoughts for Your Life's Journey,* encourages you on your journey towards being your authentic self. Full of great advice, this workbook puts the power in your hands to make different choices in thought and behaviour to change your life. As Ruth says, you were not born a winner, nor were you born a loser; you were born a chooser. *Choose* to read this book.

Karen Degen - Author of 'Heightening Your Happiness -
How you can develop the skill of enjoying your life'

I have read Ruth's book, *Musings of a Blogger – Inspirational Thoughts for Your Life's* Journey, and was very excited to see this is aimed at the individual who needs to embrace change, to enhance their lives, move outside of their comfort zone and, break through the *"terror Barrier".* It has often been said that your goal or your dream is on the other side of your fear - this book exemplifies that and goes one step further and, simplifies it! A *must read* for all those who need to make changes in their direction and live the life of their dreams.

Great work Ruth. God Bless.

Bruce Vesey-Brown - Home Based Business Specialist,
Independant Jeunesse Distributer

Musings of a Blogger

Inspirational Thoughts for Your Life's Journey

R U T H   A N N E   C A U K W E L L

BALBOA.
PRESS

A DIVISION OF HAY HOUSE

Balboa Press books may be ordered through booksellers or by contacting:

Balboa Press
A Division of Hay House
1663 Liberty Drive
Bloomington, IN 47403
www.balboapress.com.au
1 (877) 407-4847

Print information available on the last page.

ISBN: 978-1-5043-0049-0 (sc)
ISBN: 978-1-5043-0050-6 (e)

Balboa Press rev. date: 01/06/2016

To my best supporter and friend, Marie Caukwell

Mum dear, thank you for your unceasing love and belief in me. Without that, and *you*, this book would never have happened!

Your journey will consist of many small steps and not one giant one—so step forwards in confidence and with courage towards your future.

Contents

Introduction

How this book came to be written

I wrote this book from my inspirational blog, RuAnCa.blogspot.co.nz, which I started in January 2015, after I had gone through a soul-destroying period of adult bullying, one from which I thought I would never recover. Time and support did heal me, though, and because of these experiences, I learned a lot about myself—who I thought I was, *not* who I *really* was! I had prided myself that I was a strong woman able to cope with anything. I had come out of a number of traumatic events earlier in my life and had moved on. Little did I realize that all I had done was bury my hurt, pain, and authentic self through busyness and work and was living with a sense of numbness behind a thick wall of self-preservation. The bullying was the straw that broke the camel's back, and I was broken both physically and mentally.

As I started to heal, I was inspired to write my blog and e-books about women. My blog took off, and I found myself part of a network of people who appreciated and were supported by my heartfelt words. Suddenly, I felt like a caterpillar released from my own chrysalis—a chrysalis of hurt, pain, and hiding—and I was ready to fly above the ugliness of those people who would trample me down. I was ready to fly like a butterfly, high above, into the clouds of life, and burst forth from my chrysalis of hurt, but changed and renewed, ready to live again!

Just as the caterpillar goes through its own personal cycle of life, turning into a chrysalis and then bursting out of its protective shell into a wondrous butterfly—one of the most beautiful of God's creatures on this earth—I hope that this inspirational book will aid you in bursting out of your protective chrysalis and becoming such a being, beautiful and unique, able to spread your wings, soak up the sun of life, and *fly free*.

Go forth, dear reader. Burst free and live again. Live your life to the fullest!

With love,
Ruth Anne Caukwell

Suggestions to my readers on how to use this book

Have you ever noticed how children see things differently—oh so simply? Nothing is complicated and involved, plus they bounce back and forgive so easily. They know what they want and let things go, seemingly without remorse and complications. Why is it that once we reach adulthood, things change? Everything becomes more complicated then. We find it hard to forgive, let go, and move on—instead, we *think* too much about things, mull them over, and because of this, they become part of our inner selves. We build walls that will keep us safe while hiding behind masks,[1] pretending that we are okay. We also take on board other people's words, actions, and treatment of us, making them so much part of ourselves that sadly they become entrenched within our psyches, ultimately changing who we are and burying our authentic selves. But I have great news: this book, *Musings of a Blogger*, will change all of this.

When you immerse yourself within its pages, you will come to realize just how much circumstances and people influence your life, both in negative and positive ways. It's good news because if you work through the workbook utilizing the tools that are applicable for you, you can begin a journey of self-discovery. You will start to recognize that within yourself is a wonderful, unique human being, and through perseverance, you will find your true self again—your own authentic self! How wonderful is that?

There are four ways that *Musings of a Blogger* can be utilized, but before you begin, I recommend that you read Part 1 first and then flick through the workbook in Part 2. I suggest that you take some time thinking about the content and it applies to you! When, and only when, you are ready, reread Part 1. Follow the exercises in the workbook, either in conjunction with each chapter as it is read or when Part 1 has been reread in its entirety. Concentrate on those topics that you feel are more applicable to you—those that touch your inner self—rather than just

---

[1]   Refer to chapter 7, "The masks that we wear"

working your way through them all. If you feel comfortable working your way through the entire book, great!

1. Read *Musings of a Blogger* on your own and when you are ready, reread it and work through the workbook.
2. You can follow the process as mentioned above, but instead of by yourself, read it with someone you trust, either working through the workbook separately or, if comfortable, together.
3. You can read the book within a reading group—again, either working through the workbook separately and in private or, if comfortable, within the group. There is also the option of discussing the reading group questions posed at the end and/or adding your own reading group questions to the mix!
4. You can read *Musings of a Blogger*, have a quick look at the workbook, and then place it in your bookshelf amongst your other books, to gather dust and be forgotten.

I know just how hard it is to start and continue on a journey of self-discovery and reflection. It can sometimes be just too hard, too painful, too confronting. *That's okay*! Make a start, have a look through the pages to familiarize yourself with the content, and if you feel that at any time it is becoming too confronting, put the book aside. Have a rest from it but do return to it and do work through it, no matter how long it takes. On page 157 there is space for you to write any ideas, thoughts or what comes to mind while reading Part 1 and working through Part 2.

Make yourself a folder and decorate it with pictures and sayings that you like and can identify with. Then photocopy the workbook pages so that you can return to any work that you started, revisiting the same questions again. You will then have space/unwritten pages of the workbook to work with. Most importantly, date and sign each entry so you can see just how far you have come in your journey of discovery. Then fill in the certificate of achievement so that you can be proud of what you have achieved.

You can find your authentic self—the choice is yours.
You were born great.
You were born authentic.
You were born with everything you need because you are you.
You are an individual.
You are unique and nobody else can be you,
So believe in yourself and take those steps forwards.
Go out there and make your journey of life your own!

The Hexagon of Life

The Hexagon of Life

I call the repeated design within this book the hexagon of life. It consists of a hexagon with tipped points, dots around the outside, and a butterfly within. All of these components are very symbolic and together make up a profound image and clear meaning for life.

1 – Each of the hexagon's six sides represents a vital part of existence and when combined forms the basis of a well-rounded life:

- physical
- spiritual
- emotional
- relationships and social
- leisure
- environment

One or more of these components may be missing, reflected in a negative way, or detrimental to your physical and mental well-being—or maybe there is a period within your life of extra stress such as any of the following:

- eating an unhealthy diet and/or not exercising
- not taking time out to relax and do anything we enjoy doing
- being involved in an abusive relationship
- having a loved one die
- losing a job

If this is the case, the hexagon will not be a hexagon. The same goes for your life. If one of these components is out of sync or missing, there will be an unbalance—a gap—thereby leaving you vulnerable, defenceless, and open to hurt, pain, suffering, and living an unhealthy life, either mentally physically or both.

2 – The points on the hexagon represent the antennae of the butterfly, one of the most important physical characteristics of their bodies, as the nerve endings in them transmit messages to their brains. At the base of each antenna is the Johnston's organ, used for balance and orientation. Without it, the butterfly cannot fly (Edwards 2008). The same is true for you. If your life is out of balance and orientated towards the negative, you will not be able to fly free! Your thoughts, self-talk, feelings, and ultimately actions will be transmitted in a negative way, and you will struggle with living a fulfilled balanced life—one full of positivity and happiness.

3 – The dots around the hexagon represent the markings on butterflies' wings, which help to camouflage them, while the bright colours are there to warn off predators (Edwards 2008). These are representative of your camouflages, which could be in the form of your words, thoughts, beliefs, actions, and masks. These are the things that you believe, wear, or show to others to hide your inner hurt, pain, and ultimately your authentic self.

4 – The butterfly within the hexagon represents freedom; it represents you. Just as the butterfly can break out of its chrysalis and fly free, so can you. You just need the tools to help you change your life. Contained within this book are tools that will assist you in making positive changes in your life. The choice is yours!

Note: The hexagon of life was designed from a concept running around in my head, by Marie Doris Caukwell, poet and artist.

Part 1

Musings of a Blogger

1 – Do you have a dream?

Go confidently in the direction of your dreams!
Live the life you have imagined.
—Goethe

Do you have a dream? Have you written it down, drawn around it in bright colours, and written a date beside it? Is it a concrete dream or just an airy-fairy thought or group of thoughts?

Is life too busy, stressful, or hard for you so it's easier to shove your dream away in the depths of you mind?

Are there too many of life's obstacles in the way? Perhaps you feel that you are old, have too many children, not enough money, or not enough encouragement. The list goes on and on!

Most people never get what they really truly want out of life because they do not know for sure what it is. They make excuses, let things crowd in, or lose their dreams within the storms of life.

Stop.
Take a minute to have hope.

Be optimistic and just hang in there.
Take everything in your life one step at a time.

Never be willing to settle for whatever has come or comes your way and ask yourself, by spending time with yourself, what makes your soul sing. What is it that you truly want? Ask yourself these questions:

- What make me feel the most alive?
- What were my dreams when I was a child?
- What would I do if I had the confidence to follow my dreams?

Make a list of questions that suit you and then answer them. As you unearth, discover, and write down your dreams, the ones that make you feel excited and motivated, you will become responsive to bringing about change in your life so that you can begin. Do you want to make a start in achieving what you want? Do you want to start a journey to your dreams?

> A smooth sea never made a skilled mariner.
> —English proverb

On every journey within your life, obstacles will arise, but be determined to make the very best choices that you can. Grow from any difficulties and slay those demons.[2] Whether these demons are real (such as lack of finances), imagined (such as feeling that you are not worthy of success), or seemingly out of your control (such as difficulties breaking into the career of your choice), have faith, as there will be a way to break them down and continue with your dream. Go forth into the days ahead with a steadfast belief and hope that things will work out okay.

- Count your blessings.
- Climb those ladders.
- Be strong and be patient.
- Use wisdom to make those right choices.[3]
- Seek and surround yourself with the right people for you and your dreams.
- Do some soul-searching.
- Acknowledge what might be holding you back and look at those excuses.
- Realize that you have an incredible amount of power. It's all in your own hands when it comes to directing your life!

---

[2] Refer to chapter 2, "The stoppers in our lives"
[3] Refer to chapter 10, "Choices, chances, and changes"

Yes, circumstances and life crowd in. Fear can rule your mind, procrastination can shape your day, and challenges can arise that will suck you dry, but take a deep breath and break through your fears![4]

Continue on your journey of life and move towards those dreams. Do not wait for that knight in shining armour to slay the dragon of indecision and fear. Instead, do it yourself! Believe in your dreams, believe in your happy ending, for it is in your hands. You are the author of your own story. Go forth and follow your dreams!

The journey of a thousand miles begins with a single step.
—Chinese proverb

Success is a journey, not a destination.
—Anonymous

---

[4]   Refer to chapter 3, "What is fear?"

2 – The stoppers in our lives

It is not who you are, what you have, or where you live that makes you happy or unhappy. It is what and how you think, act, and feel about yourself. These are the stoppers, the plugs, that limit you and your freedom to be happy. Let go of them now.

Today I had an appointment, and afterwards, to replenish my soul, I went to sit by the seaside to reflect and think things through. Oh, how beautiful it was! After some days of stormy weather, the sea was rough and wild. The waves were crashing and the wind howling a real breeze. What was so amazingly wonderful was that due to the storms, huge piles of seaweed had been washed up on the shore, some still coming in and going out with the movement of the tide.

A number of the piles of seaweed had huge stumps on the bottom and tree-like trunks, some with one, two, and even three emerging from them. They looked like giant plugs at the base, and emerging from the tree-like "trunks" were a myriad of tangled, wild, and rambling "branches." Some were thick, some were thin, and others were so fine that they looked like filigrees of handmade lace.

Walking amongst this amazing spectacle whilst watching the waves crash onto the shore, with the seagulls picking and scrambling amongst these washed-up giants, I wondered where they had come from and thought how majestic they must have looked in life with their forms floating upwards under the ocean and swaying in the currents! What fish, what creatures, must have passed them by? How old were they? What had they seen? If they could speak, what could they have said? If they could hear what would they have heard? But sadly, I would get nothing out of them because they lay on the beach with their majesty and glory dulled and dying now that they were out on dry land, but they still had magnificent beauty! I saw that beauty still. I saw that beauty in what they represented to me.

To me, they represented the plugs, the stoppers, that we have within our lives—the bases upon where we often plant our feet and from there let our whole existence emerge and grow, but not in a healthy way. Instead, these plugs, these stoppers, bung up, stunt, and stop who we really are. They limit our growth as people, pushing us to become what we are not and systematically helping to bury our authentic selves in the process. These plugs might include the following:

- sadness
- anger
- resentment
- hatred
- apathy and procrastination
- regret
- jealousy
- perfectionism

The list goes on and may even include people. However, these huge plugs, with their tree-like "trunks" and numerous branches, had been pulled up off the sea floor where they had been born, lived their lives, been fed, and grown, seemingly there forever. Now they were just lying there devoid of life, as they had become lost in the wild and stormy sea, just as we can be.

Sometimes we get lost when we take a wrong turning. We allow the plugs to bung up all those good things open to us, and we let them stop our lives from blossoming.

So, my reader, take a moment out of your busy life and look for those stoppers that keep you from growing into the most wonderful human being that you were meant to be. Once you find them, pull them up out of your life, where they were born, fed, grown, and now live. You have the strength and courage to take that step and pull the plug on your stoppers.

Your life is a journey, and it is up to you which path you take and in what direction you move. You can be like a fern frond, tightly rolled up and closed, or you can open up to the good things in life. Make up your mind. You can do it!

3 – What is fear?

Why walk hand in hand with fear when you can let go and walk through it?

What is fear? That's a difficult question to answer, for it means a different thing to each of us. There are fears arising from such aspects as danger, expectation of pain, and physical events, which are natural responses, but what about those personal acknowledged and unacknowledged fears—and those hidden fears? Fears are caused by such things as the following:

- judgement
- opinions of others
- incorrect thinking of "self"
- destructive self-talk
- self-doubt
- not being good enough—beautiful or handsome, rich, or educated enough
- not being perfect
- being weak
- change[5]

---

[5]   Refer to chapter 4, "Embrace change"

- making decisions and choices[6]
- the future

The list goes on and on!

Dear reader, you know what fears I mean. They are those fears that you identify with. They are those fears that are there but not acknowledged—all those fears that are within you, the ones behind that wall, the ones that you keep hidden. Maybe you act upon those fears through such things as the following:

- Procrastination
- keeping busy
- perfectionism
- anger
- shyness
- bullying
- low self-esteem[7]

Once again, this list is inexhaustible. I am sure you can think of so many more fears with which you can identify.

Sadly, our thought patterns, inner images, and ultimately our lives can be ruled by any or all of these types of fears.[8] Our inner images are the private pictures that we have of ourselves and those that reflect our own thoughts, feelings, and actions, all of which we mostly keep within. To hide them, we often put on masks[9] that help us cope with life, situations, people, and those inner fears.

Our outer images are the public pictures that we portray outwardly for others to see. These images are more often than not so very different from our inner images and are ones that we start to build upon from childhood and throughout our lives.[10] However, we can end up neglecting and ignoring our inner selves and instead nourish, care for, and tend to our outer images—and the result? We end up living behind walls and feeling empty inside.

If we live behind these walls, we will find ourselves living with and through our fears. But if we choose to break through these walls, we will instead be able to face our fears.

---

[6] Refer to chapter 10, "Choices, chances, and changes"
[7] Refer to chapter 5, "Self-esteem—what are your values?"
[8] Refer to chapter 3, "What is fear?"
[9] Refer to chapter 7, "The masks that we wear"
[10] Refer to chapter 6, "Challenge your thought patterns"

Everything you want is ultimately on the other side of fear, as fear obscures our vision and we begin to only see our limitations. Be an explorer, for the world is filled with so much wonder and magical things.

Life is a promise, and our real voyages of discovery lie not in hiding from our fears or seeing with obscured eyes. Instead, they lie in stepping out with faith, confidence, belief, and having new eyes to see. To step out, we need to acknowledge our fears. We need to recognize them and step through what we fear, going forwards against those contrary beliefs that swirl within our minds. Never turn back. Press onwards until you have overcome.

Even though this may seem so difficult at times, if you truly look inwards, you will become aware of the resources that you have, and therein lies the power to overcome your fears.

Dear reader, my wish for you is to live a fulfilling life, one where you can be your authentic self and live not in fear but in peace, happiness, and love.

May your journey of discovery be free of fear!

4 – Embrace change

Perhaps you are wondering why you should embrace change. Change is difficult, and you might be afraid. Yes, change can be hard to cope with, but when you look back on your life's journey and realise that you have not moved further than your own backyard, how difficult will that be to live with?

Change![11] What is it? What does it mean? According to the *Reader's Digest Oxford Complete Wordfinder*, "change" means the following: *1 a* the act or an instance of making or becoming different. *b* an alteration or modification *(the change in her expression)*.

Yes, it is inevitable that change will occur within our lives, and when it occurs, it often happens in directions that we would never have imagined. Sometimes we can cope with and look forward to change, but sometimes it is difficult to deal with and can cause conflict, making us dread it.

Change touches us in so many ways and through so many things—more than can ever be mentioned here—and it can occur worldwide, socially, with family, or for personal reasons. However, our circumstances, attitudes, and choices determine how much we let change affect us. For every change that occurs in our lives, whether we seem to cope with it or not, we will be strengthened if we let

---

[11]   Refer to chapter 10, "Choices, chances, and changes"

it, ready for the next change to come. It is not the way of life to live without knowing a storm or two, and for every struggle, whether internal or external, we will experience change.

Change can either strengthen or defeat. But change is good because growth, strength, and courage are not won through the absence of conflict, whether internal or external. It instead comes from the ability to look at and deal with change!

Change can touch each of us in varying ways, sometimes hardly at all but sometimes so personally that one's very essence itself is affected.

The only person each of us is destined to be is the person that we decide that we want to be and it is how we deal with the changes that come within our voyages of life that makes us that person. It is our choices,[12] as much as the paths and opportunities we take or ignore, that influence the manner with which we deal with change. So each day look around and be happy with the choices that you have made in your life and the changes that have come from them.

Choices influence change, and change influences our lives. So embrace change, as change ultimately makes our voyages of life and discovery complete. It shapes the way it was meant to be for each of us!

> The real voyage of discovery lies not in seeking new landscapes, but in having new eyes.
> —Marcel Proust

---

[12]   Refer to chapter 10, "Choices, chances, and changes"

5 – Self-esteem—what are your values?

Just what is self-esteem? Self-esteem is the value that you place on yourself. And it is that value that determines your ability to experience satisfaction in your life. The extent to which you can value yourself is influenced and a product of past experiences such as the following:

- Your successes and failures (as you perceive them)
- The support and recognition you receive from others, especially those who have played an important part or who are significant in your life now
- The support, love, and recognition (or maybe lack of it) that you received in your younger years

All of these aspects influence how and what you feel about yourself right now—your self-esteem, your self-worth, your beliefs, and your actions. You can only love yourself to the extent that you know how and to the extent that you have been loved. You are only able to love others to the extent that you love yourself. How telling this is!

So in a nutshell, depending on whatever your self-esteem is—low, medium, or high—and depending on what your self beliefs are, they all reflect how negatively or positively you see, think, and talk to yourself. Perhaps you have limiting beliefs such as the following:[13]

- I'm too young/too old.
- I'm too fat/too thin.
- I'm a woman/a man.
- I'm the wrong culture.
- I'm too rich/too poor.
- I'm too dumb; I don't have the education.
- I'm not perfect enough; I've failed.
- I've had a bad childhood.

Are you holding on to these limiting beliefs as tightly as you can? Are you letting negative self-talk sabotage your future? Are you stuck because of fear?[14] Do you hide behind a wall of hurt, with no gate to get out? Is this you? If it is, think about these four aspects: your beliefs, self-talk, feelings, and actions. All of these are cyclical in nature, with one leading to another, to another, to another.

If you have limiting or negative beliefs, your self-talk will be limiting or negative, your feelings will be limiting or negative, and your actions will be limiting or negative. This cycle will go on and on throughout your life. It will ruin your happiness,[15] your success, and your ability to love. You will never be truly free. The uniqueness of yourself will be lost in a negative cloud of false belief, self-talk, feelings, and actions! So instead confront that belief, that self-talk, that feeling, that action—and believe in yourself!

You are a unique human being. There is no one else in the world, in the universe, like you. You are very special. You are a one of a kind here in this world—here in this time and space—and therefore you are worth your loving yourself!

You are as unique as the young butterfly who flaps her wings for the first time, the single blade of grass that sways and bends against the wind, the newborn baby who cries for his mother. Be proud of yourself and of who you are!

> One of the hardest lessons you will learn in life is learning to believe in yourself.
> Once you get that, you will realize that you are capable of anything.
> —Steven Aitchison

---

[13] Refer to chapter 6, "Challenge Your Thought Patterns"
[14] Refer to chapter 3, "What is fear?"
[15] Refer to chapter 9, "We can all have happiness—so just go out and grab it!"

When you look long into an abyss, the abyss also looks into you.
—Friedrich Nietzsche

Take a moment to read these questions and think about them, deeply and with conviction:

- When you look inwardly at yourself, what do you really see?
- What do you think of yourself?
- Do you know who you are?
- Do you see yourself one way, but your loved ones, friends and colleagues see you another way?
- Who is the real you—the way you see yourself or the way others see you?

Disappointments and happenings can often take you down a path that you would not have chosen for yourself. Dreams and desires can be lost in a maelstrom of chaos, where your authentic self can get overwhelmed and buried. Life and events can threaten to sweep you away and you lose sight of who you really are. You can begin to form negative tapes, judge yourself, and fall into negative patterns, resulting in negative thoughts, negative self-talk, negative beliefs about yourself.

Some of these negative aspects may have been dormant from childhood or formed in teenage or early adult years. They surface at times, only to be pushed back down again, but they keep emerging from time to time, when there is a build-up of stress and anxiety, or they just lie there under the surface, subconsciously dragging you down. Some are formed as you travel through the storms of life or are piled on top of those negative aspects that have already been formed.

Do you play-act through life with a false attitude and image, hiding negative self-talk, feelings, actions, hurt, and pain behind a wall?[16] Do you cover up how you feel and who you really are? If you are not sure, just think of the many ways that there are of covering up feelings:

- Do you become aggressive and loud?
- Do you bluster and bully your way through life?
- Are you a doormat or a cowering mouse?
- Do you push your way through to the front or do you creep in and sit at the back?
- Do you hide away from life and people?
- Do you accept other people's treatment of you, never fighting back and standing up for yourself?
- Can you say no?

Can you identify with any of these? Or maybe you use other ways ... How do you cover up your feelings? What are your negative tapes? Do you even know? If not, please sit down with a pen and paper in your hand and start to think about them. Start to challenge them as these negative tapes,[17] which if not recognized and challenged, will stunt your growth because all the experiences we go through and what we put into our minds helps form the ideas that we have, the judgements that we make, and the value that we place upon ourselves as human beings.

Sadly, many of these are filled with incorrect data consisting of only opinions that we form about ourselves, not true facts. They are not true facts about ourselves and who we really are. Instead, they are just opinions that enable us to set up all sorts of barriers for ourselves based upon incorrect data—data that is perceived and not real.

Our thought patterns and self-talk help form our beliefs, and they are two of the most important things that dictate our behaviour. These are then reflected in each other and thus form a cycle that goes round and round. Behaviour equals belief equals behaviour equals belief equals behaviour.

---

16   Refer to chapter 7, "The masks that we wear"
17   Refer to chapter 6, "Challenge your thought patterns"

This never-ending cycle forces us into a circle of thinking patterns that, if filled with negativity, lead us into low self-esteem, in turn feeding the cycle … with negative food.

Do you want to live your life this way? Do you want to be controlled by your negative tapes? Do you want to live your life not doing things that you are capable of? Do you want to live your life behind a wall? Do you really want to continue going through life fooling yourself with perceived opinions and not living it through real facts? Ask yourself today. Decide today. Is it authenticity and real facts or is it negative tapes and perceived opinions by which you want to live?

Challenge your thought patterns now. In truth may you walk and in truth may you live! Through all the returning seasons, may you grow and change just as summer turns into spring and spring into autumn and autumn into winter. May you move and grow with life, singing with the birds, walking through the trails marked with ferns and trees, with flowers blooming fresh and snow falling thick. May you live with truth and let truth lead you, guide you, and help you live your life to the full! You were born in truth. Let you live in truth and finish in truth!

Decide today whether you will live by perceived opinions about yourself or in real facts. Take some time to look at what you think about yourself and ask yourself some hard questions. Do you have negative tapes? Challenge your thinking and discover a new authentic you!

7 – The Masks We Wear

At some time or another, we all wear masks—not physical masks but social masks—that we put on before leaving the house to disguise or hide what we are truly feeling inside.

The *Reader's Digest Oxford Complete Wordfinder* defines "mask" in this way:

1 a a covering for all or part of the face:

4 disguise, guise, camouflage, show, semblance, pretence, cover, cover-up, false colours, concealment, cloak, façade, veil.

Why do we feel we have to don those masks? Why do we feel that we cannot just be ourselves? And why do we not have enough faith in ourselves to believe that we are just as good as the next person?

> Believe in yourself! Have faith in your abilities! Without a humble but reasonable
> confidence in your own powers you cannot be successful or happy.
> —Norman Vincent Peale

These are such true words!

Yes, all of us can wear masks to hide a fear of not fitting in, whether at a party or other social setting, at work, in a business meeting, in the classroom, and sadly, even within our own families. Or we can wear masks to hide the truth of being abused, feelings of loneliness,[18] lack of confidence, grief and expressing that grief to others, being sick, being unhappy, being suicidal, or being unfaithful.

Why are we afraid and wear these masks? Are we afraid of being hurt further, of not fitting in, of being belittled? Are we ashamed or *what*?[19]

Inside, we can be crying, lonely, heartbroken, and full of despair, but on the outside, we are carefree, laughing, and happy-go-lucky, wearing those masks to cover up and pretend.

Masks

We all wear a thousand faces and hide the one that's real.
We present an unruffled composure and don't show what we feel.
Beneath that smiling exterior, we hide our hurts and fears.
We shy away from contact so no one can see our tears.
We chat amiably to each other, not really caring to dig,
as we feel we cannot deal with the hurts that we'd reveal.
But, dear friend, God gave us the gift, through love, to heal;
If only we would try to listen and look behind the mask.
A hug, a word, a moment shared—sometimes that's all that's needed.
The springs break up, and the hurt is healed, so let us really listen and
Hear what is not being said,
Using our hearts' compassion to show others we care.
—Marie Caukwell

As caring people, let us begin to look behind the facade that people present and not take them at face value. Instead, take a moment or two to listen and look behind that smile, laughter, and brightness. We just might get a glimpse of hidden pain, unhappiness, loneliness, or some other hurt. It need only take us a moment to forget ourselves and see the mask that is being worn, hiding or covering up something. Then we can give a hug, hold a hand, say a kind word, and be there for that person.

---

[18]   Refer to chapter 8, "Loneliness and hope"
[19]   Refer to chapter 2, "Stoppers in our lives"

The call to simplicity and freedom is a reminder that our worth comes not from the amount of our involvements, achievements, or possessions, but from the depth and care which we bring to each moment, place, and person in our lives.
—Richard A. Bower

Dear reader, my hope for you today and every day is that if you are wearing a mask, throw it away and let us meet each other face-to-face, with honesty and compassion. Have the confidence to be who you are and be proud. Go out there and embrace you. Embrace your personality, looks, feelings and your whole life.[20] If you need support, do not be afraid to seek it. If you are hurting, do not be afraid to say so. Remember that you are worth it!

---

[20] Refer to chapter 4, "Embrace change"

Hope costs nothing.
—Colette

Loneliness. The very sound of the word has a haunting quality! How it can tug at one's heart, leaving an echo of emptiness. Loneliness is everywhere and can be found anywhere, whether on a crowded bus, in a restaurant, at a party, in a schoolroom, at work, and even within a family. You can be alone in the wilderness but also lonely amongst a multitude, as loneliness can be vastly different from being alone.

One of the *Reader's Digest Oxford Complete Wordfinder* definitions for "alone" is as follows: *1 a.* without others present *b.* without others' help; and "loneliness" is defined this way: lonesomeness, aloneness, solitude, desolation, isolation and seclusion.

You can be alone yet be happy and contented, but being lonely can be like a virus, insidious as it creeps up on you, or it can strike you to an unusual extent, and often there is no control over it. Loneliness is impartial to who you are or what you have. It can strike anybody, whether a person is rich or poor, lives on the streets or in a mansion, is single or partnered, has ten children or has none, or works as a businessperson or a cashier.

Many of us have experienced adversity, pain, and sorrow, which often brings on loneliness and which can sometimes fill our whole being, bring us to our knees, and make life seem worthless. But as hard as it is, we must ride through the loneliness and those negative feelings, for loneliness does not have to be forever or rule your life.

If you realise that the setbacks in your life are a turning point to something better, the universe will be open to you. If you can turn your life around and live in hope, you will see and know the richness that people and life have to offer! So instead of living with loneliness, reach out! Hold on to hope for the following reasons:

- Hope can move mountains.
- Hope is what has saved many a person who has gone through the most horrific of times.
- Hope is innate within us all, even you!
- Hope is your lifeline to overcome.
- Hope is the beginning of you changing your own world and your own circumstances.[21]

Live and nurture hope, and then you will be able to conquer anything, including loneliness. The tapestry of a life lived with hope lets you anticipate what that life can be. Use that hope to reach out and grasp life, negate loneliness, and to ask for help, even if you can only take baby steps at first.

Do grasp hold of your innate hope, your own life, and take a chance to change the way you think and do. Live with hope and use it to overcome anything and everything. You are a unique human being. There is no one else like you in the universe. It will not be easy, and you will have to work at it, but have faith in yourself to overcome!

Take heart, dear reader, and trust yourself! You can start the next chapter of your life by just discarding the old negative ones and live with wonderful new positive ones. This in itself brings hope.

> Change your thoughts and you change your world.
> —Norman Vincent Peale

> Great things are not done by impulse but by a series of small things brought together.
> —Vincent van Gogh

---

[21] Refer to chapter 10, "Choices, chances, and changes"

Nothing can bring you happiness but yourself.
—Ralph Waldo Emerson

Happiness allows us to feel hope when we are in despair. Happiness gives us peace in a world of turmoil. Happiness allows us to dream and gives us peace. Happiness is one of the most beautiful feelings that we can have, so go out and grab it with both hands! It is within your reach, and you can attain it.

But what is this thing called happiness? If you look in the *Reader's Digest Oxford Complete Wordfinder*, "happiness" is defined as the following: pleasure, delight, enjoyment, joy, joyfulness, jubilation, cheerfulness and exhilaration.

However, this definition cannot fully explain just what happiness is. Yes, it is a feeling, and yes, these words describe part of what happiness is, but it is so much more.

A great motto to live by each day is this: Today is wonderful. It is my choice to celebrate my life and be happy! Today is a present to enjoy—so live as though each day is wonderful and good just because you are alive. You have a free choice to be happy or not to be happy.

A man [or woman] is [can be] happy so long as he [or she] chooses
to be happy and nothing can stop him [or her].
—Alexander Solzhenitsyn

It is not what you possess, who you are, how much money you have, where you live, whether you are single or attached, the type of education and how much you have, the number of friends you have, the success of your career, or your circumstances in life. None of these, or even a mixture of them, can make you totally happy or unhappy. Oh, yes, all or some of them can and will attribute to that feeling people call happiness, but if you are reliant on these things or other people to attain true happiness, then you will never attain it. But it is not that hard to have true happiness; it is not that complicated. It is basically what and how you think, feel, and act about yourself and your life. That is the key to it all!

If you seek to be happy by looking at and trying to be just like others, you are not being true to yourself. If you keep looking at the following, how dissatisfied you will become:

- at another person's possessions;
- at the false beauty of others you see all around you;
- at those who have more education than yourself or went to better schools;
- at those who seem to have more friends than you; or
- at the fame and fortune that some people have and you do not.

When this occurs, you will not recognize the beauty of what you have inside of you and who you are. Instead, these will be buried and pushed aside for the unrealistic needs and wants of the world around you; sadly, self-doubt and wishing will tarnish those wonderful aspects of your authentic self. They will be lost forever!

How do you know what the rich person's thoughts really are? Just think about that for a moment. He or she could look at you and your life, wishing for what you have.

How do you know what those beautiful people feel?

How do you know what fame and fortune really does to a person? Maybe he/she looks at your life and who you are, with envy?

You can travel the world searching for happiness and maybe you will find it after an age. But because the world is round, you will eventually return to where you started and find your happiness was right there, sitting at your own back door!

Sometimes we think that the following will bring us that happiness we want and deserve:

- lots of friends, a partner, and children
- having education and a successful career
- a particular place, possessions, a big house, and money

But often when we get the things that we desire, we find that they are filled with flaws instead, as we cannot buy, own, or have someone else make us happy! When we start to realize this, it is time to begin to search within yourself and find out what it is that will really bring you true happiness.

Yes, happiness can be attainable for all of us. But the ultimate reality of it is that there is only one person who can bring you happiness, and that is you yourself. No one else can do it for you! So by changing your thoughts, you can change your world!

Dear reader, when you open your eyes each morning, say to yourself, "Today is wonderful. It is my choice to celebrate my life and be happy!" My wish for you is to find and be your authentic self and be happy[22] today and every day!

> It isn't what you have, or who you are, or where you are, or what you are
> doing that makes you happy or unhappy. It is what you think about.
> —Dale Carnegie

---

[22]   Refer to chapter 9, "We can all have happiness—so just go out and grab it!"

You do not have to stay behind your wall.
You can build a gate instead and go through it.

What is life? Many people have asked this question since the beginning of time, but who among us can really answer in a way that explains just what it is? Yes, life is physical, mental, spiritual, and the feeling of sensations—hearing, seeing, and thinking—that we experience. However, life is more than that. Life is also a journey, and for each of us, it is a destination. So your life is your destination!

From the day you were born until the day you pass over, you are travelling on a journey to reach your own destination! To where? With whom? For how long?

We don't know the answers to these questions. Not even our parents, grandparents, siblings, friends, teachers, partners, colleagues, or even strangers can tell us where we each are heading.

Sure, all of us are influenced by our upbringings, cultures, ethnicities, religions, societies, and by others. But the reality of it is that no one can tell you where you are going or what your journey will entail. Others do not know our destination. In fact, we ourselves do not even know! How exciting is that!

Life is a journey, a destination, but it is also a journey of discovery. You are the traveller as you travel the journey of life. You make the choices. You take the chances. You live the changes.[23]

Dear readers, none of you were born winners, but you were not born losers either. You were born choosers. So take a chance and choose to be winners. Choose to be happy, no matter what! Choose to make those decisions that fulfil you and make your life good.

Life and circumstances can dictate how you feel, what you do, and all your thoughts and feelings, but ultimately it is up to you too.[24]

Choose to make your own journey one of purpose, power, and strength. Choose and take the chance to change what needs changing.

> You must make a choice to take a chance or your life will never change.
> —Michael Baisden

If contrary winds blow strong in your face, go forwards, never turning back. Instead continue to press forwards, onwards, and upwards, as you do not need to have a lot of might to be victorious. Your life is a journey, a destination, but in the travelling you, have the choice to take the chances to make those changes that are necessary to live the best life possible for you.

May peace and stillness be with you in your journey of life!

> We do not receive wisdom; we must discover it for ourselves after
> a journey that no one can take for us or spare us.
> —Marcel Proust

---

23   Refer to chapter 4, "Embrace change"
24   Refer to chapter 1, "Do you have a dream?"

Part 2

Workbook

"The Parable of the Butterfly"

"The Parable of the Butterfly"

"The Parable of the Butterfly" has been around for a while, and you can find many versions online. This version is how I perceive the story and how it applies to life. This parable is applicable to all of us and how we live our lives. I hope that you enjoy reading it.

> A little boy lived with his mother in a small house with a beautiful garden. Most days after school, the little boy would sit under his favourite tree with his mother and they would talk about his day.
>
> It was on one of these occasions that the little boy noticed a number of butterflies resting on a nearby bush, slowly moving their wings. Running to the bush, he saw that all but one of the cocoons hanging there was empty. Wanting to find out why, he bent closer to look at the single cocoon.
>
> The little boy noticed a butterfly trying to emerge from the cocoon. Wanting to help, he pried open the casing and freed the struggling insect, which fell to the ground. He watched as the butterfly moved feebly, too weak to rise and fly away.
>
> Devastated, the little boy realized that the butterfly needed the struggle in order to strengthen its wings to be able to fly free from the cocoon.

All of us awaken in the morning and move through the day with our own personal thoughts, feelings, and actions, but we also share these hours with others. Each day that we have is given to us, and we can either rely totally on those we walk alongside or recognize that within ourselves—with all the struggles, hard times, and sorrows—we can grow, become strengthened, and live fulfilled and happy lives.

Walking alongside others instead of totally relying on them allows you to become strengthened. It allows you to become who you really are, able to find your authentic self and fly free. It allows you to be who you were meant to be!

Pre-characteristics list

Vincent van Gogh knew what he was saying when he said that great things are not done by impulse but by a series of small things brought together.

Take the time to reflect on exactly what he was meaning and then think about yourself in this context and in the context of this book. When we desire something, hard work is required to achieve what we want, and often the only way to gain it is to take those steps necessary to have it come to us, whether it is any of the following:

- purchasing an item, even if it is via layaway or credit—you still have to make payments over months or years, until it is really yours. That includes buying a house. You have to make mortgage payments for years before you can call the property your own.
- studying for that certificate, degree, or some form of education—you have to study for months or years, do assignments, and pass exams so that you can go up a grade (even if you are an adult student, there is no shortcut due to age or your desired goal).
- waiting for that son or daughter to be born—there are nine months of steps to take while eating and exercising healthily, getting the nursery ready, and fitting in all those midwife/doctor's visits—and yes, even though the birth, there are steps to take.
- Once you have your child, he or she is not instantly a toddler, teenager, adult, husband/bride, father/mother. You and your child will have to wait. There are steps to take in the process of life.

The above list is endless as you move through your journey of life, and it is the same for you now as you desire to learn, grow, and discover your authentic self.

This book will help you in taking those steps, and by taking them one at a time, you will learn, grow, and discover authenticity.

You will achieve great things through a series of smaller things brought together by you. The first step in doing this is for you to recognise the positive and good that abound within yourself! So take time to fill out your pre-characteristics list and celebrate your positives. You will find it at the end of this workbook. It is a revisiting of your thoughts, opinions, and beliefs. While it is the final step within this book, it is not the final one in your life. Recognize your greatness!

You can only grow as high as you can reach. You can only travel as far as you will seek. You can only go as deep within your soul as you are willing to see, and you can only be as much as you dream[25] you want to be!

My pre-characteristics list

Have a look at the below statements and tick the ones that you feel are applicable to you at this time in your life. Be positive, think honestly about who you are, and look behind any negative feelings that you have. This is an important exercise, as it gets you thinking about yourself in a positive way. This might seem hard for you to do at first, but thinking about yourself in this way is like a seed: once planted, it germinates and begins to grow; as it is watered, it grows and grows into something more wonderful than it was before. Being positive and watering it with realisation that you are unique in this world and full of so many incredible things will help you grow more beautiful each day. It will help you realize that you are that butterfly and can fly free. Think positive!

☐ I can express gratitude for my life.

☐ I look for the good in all I do.

☐ I feel attractive because I am who I am.

☐ I have a sense of humour.

☐ I look for joy, happiness, and peace in all around me.

☐ I am *unique* and realise this.

☐ I love where I am at this moment.

☐ I am confident in who and what I am.

☐ I am a creative person because I think, feel, and have a voice.

☐ Wonderful events are happening to me *right now*.

☐ I am honest and trustworthy.

☐ I set positive boundaries for myself.

☐ I am a quiet person.

☐ I feel compassion.

☐ I wake up ready for the day.

☐ I enjoy being in the outdoors.

☐ I like to talk.

☐ I feel lovable.

☐ I am a hard worker.

☐ I enjoy sports.

☐ I always have what I need.

☐ My family is important to me.

☐ I attract abundance because I know that I deserve it.

This list is just a taste of what you are. Now it is time for you to write down some more positive things about yourself those that are not on this list. There will be plenty there. Just open your mind to yourself and you will find them. Write at least ten and then look at what you have written and ticked and be proud of them. Do not forget to sign and date them too.

☐ _____

☐ _____

☐ _____

☐ _____

☐ _____

☐ _____

☐ _____

☐ _____

- [ ] _____
- [ ] _____
- [ ] _____
- [ ] _____
- [ ] _____
- [ ] _____
- [ ] _____
- [ ] _____
- [ ] _____
- [ ] _____
- [ ] _____
- [ ] _____
- [ ] _____
- [ ] _____
- [ ] _____
- [ ] _____
- [ ] _____

Signature: _____ Date: _____

Doodles of my dreams

Here is an opportunity to think about, discover, and depict your dreams! Do it in your own way. Draw them, colour them, paint them, and let yourself go!

Doodles of my dreams

Here is an opportunity to think about, discover, and depict your dreams. Do it in your own way. Draw them, colour them, paint them, and let yourself go.

My list of dreams

Now list your dreams—those things that you really want, those that will make you happy, and those that you have always dreamed of.

1.

2.

3.

4.

5.

6.

7.

8

Steps to help me achieve my dreams

Now take your list of dreams and work out some steps to achieve your dreams—make them baby steps, realistic and doable. Put a date by each one and then sign.

In doing this, you will be discovering, acknowledging, and planning your strategies to get what you desire. Just take your desires and run with them!

1.

Signature: _____ Date: _____

2.

Signature: _____ Date: _____

3.

Signature: _____ Date: _____

4.

Signature: _____ Date: _____

My top three dreams

Now think about your list of dreams. Look at them and decide which ones are most important to you. Within your list, there could be short-term dreams, long-term dreams, or dreams that are happening right now.

But whatever kind of dreams you have listed, think about them and look at how and why they are important to you. Take some time considering this before deciding which ones are your top three dreams, the ones that mean the most to you.

Write them down in order of priority and put any information that you want beside your dream, anything that you feel is applicable to your dream. Is it short term or long term? Can you accomplish this dream on your own?

1. _____
   _____
   _____
   _____
   _____

2. _____
   _____
   _____
   _____
   _____

3. _____
   _____
   _____
   _____
   _____

Do not forget to date and sign each dream!

My top three dreams card

We have so many "cards": loyalty cards, business cards, credit cards, and shop cards. All are important in their own way, and below is your top three dreams card to fill out, laminate, and add to the pile in your wallet, purse, or bag. But put this card on the top of the pile so that you can see it first.

Your top three dreams card is very important, as it is to reminds you of your dreams. You can write anything you want on it related to your dreams. Treasure it and look at it every day, for it is to remind you of your dreams—the ones that you have chosen to work on first!

My Top Three Dreams Card	
Name:	**Date:**
1.	
2.	
3.	

My dream wall board

Now is the fun part, so just let yourself go!

You have identified, listed, and worked out the steps of all your dreams and decided upon your top three dreams. It is now time to visualize just how they will look in real life. You can do this by creating your dream wall board. This will remind you of your dreams, on a daily basis, as well help keep your positive feelings alive while you are working towards them.

1 – Hang up a board. Whether it is cardboard, cork, or a whiteboard, place it somewhere that you will see it on a daily basis.

2 – Next find objects, pictures, words, sayings, anything that depicts your dreams and how you are going to achieve them. The material you use can be gotten anywhere, from magazines, books, or the Internet. If you feel creative, why not write something, draw, paint pictures, or even cut out shapes to add to your board. Make it colourful, bright, and something that is appealing and inviting to you!

3 – If you prefer, you could design a board for each of your top three dreams separately or together. Or you could have your board for all of the dreams on your list. The choice is yours.

Just remember that this board is yours to do with want you want, as it is to remind you of your dreams. Just go for it! If you feel comfortable, tell others about them.

Constantly look at and update your board with each achievement, as each step will inspire you and you will be surprised at the ideas and thoughts that will pop into your mind!

The important aspect of having your dream wall board is that is makes the images within your mind a reality and in doing so your dreams are now more than just a fantasy, a perception! They have become instead a concrete goal for you to work towards!

When you have achieved your dreams, add new ones to your board, as dreaming is free and achieving your dreams is something to celebrate.

May you dream your dreams and let them be part of you. May your dreams become a shining example to others of what can be achieved. May your dreams become a source of pride to you and to those who love you.

12 – The Stoppers in Our Lives

Do you have stoppers or plugs in your life? Think about what is stopping you from doing things that you would love to do. What is stopping you from finding happiness, joy, and peace in your life? Why are those stoppers there? Do some deep thinking and write them down. I know that this can be a difficult task to do. Take your time—and if you need to take a break before continuing/finishing this exercise, do not be afraid of doing this because writing down aspects in your life that hinder you from being your authentic self will start you on a path of freedom from them. You will begin to recognise them for what they are and be able to work at pulling the plug!

What are the stoppers or plugs in my life? Why are they there?

1.

2.

3.

4.

5.

Stopper or plug removal!

In the previous exercise, you identified some stoppers or plugs that are hindering you in your life and why they are there, so now let's brainstorm about what you can do to remove them. Often the removal process is a difficult one, and this can be due to many factors, including how much these stoppers have become part of you and your life, but make a start! You can seek help from a trusted person and brainstorm together if that suits you. Do what is comfortable for you.

Do not forget to sign and date your work. If you need more pages, just photocopy the blank ones. When you are ready to move on, be proud of what you have done!

1. My stopper is_____

How can I work to remove it?

_____
_____
_____
_____
_____
_____

2. Will I require help?

☐ Yes

☐ No

☐ Not sure

☐ Other (*explain*):

_____
_____

3. If yes, maybe, other, from whom?

_____
_____
_____

_____

_____

_____

4. Here is a big question to think about! With what can I replace my stoppers?

☐ Positive feelings/emotions

☐ Positive self-talk

☐ Positive habits

☐ Positive people in my life

☐ Fulfilling career

The above are just some ideas that might be applicable to you. Why not think about your own replacers? Be realistic, though, and realise that small achievable steps are best—ones that you can manage. Remember that little steps will lead to giant ones.

When you have written your replacers, take a break and then come back. Then number each one, from one to whatever number you have, in importance and achievability.

☐ _____

☐ _____

☐ _____

☐ _____

☐ _____

☐ _____

☐ _____

☐ _____

☐ _____

Signature: _____ Date: _____

Letter to my stopper—instructions

The following exercise is what I call a cleansing exercise. It will help remove negativity and doubt about removing and replacing those stoppers, whether they involve certain persons, a job, money, alcohol, drugs, smoking, violence, or any feeling, emotion, behaviour.

In fact, whatever your stopper is, tell the universe as well as yourself that you are unplugging your negative stopper and replacing it with a positive instead.

In your letter, explain what the stopper is, why you are removing it, and what you are replacing it with.

Be sure to include your feelings about it but, most importantly, tell the stopper how proud you are of what you are doing (and any other positive feelings you are feeling).

You can write your letter to one, two, or more of your stoppers. Do whatever you feel comfortable with. Take your time over this and keep it private, as it is your letter!

My letter ceremony

Do the following once you have written your letter:

- Consider decorating your letter along the side, on the back, or wherever, with positive drawings or doodles. I like positive words such as *I am free; I am unique; fly away negativity.* Or consider drawing hearts or stars. It is up to you!
- Fold your letter and place it in an envelope.
- Tuck it aside somewhere safe.
- When you are ready, find a quiet time when you are not busy or in a hurry and sit down with your letter.

Hold on to your letter, close your eyes, and rid yourself of any negative feelings and emotions. Breathe deeply and say words such as the following:

"Stopper [name your stopper], I release you and let you go now! I replace you with__!"

- Still with your eyes closed and breathing calmly and deeply tear your stopper up!
- Open your eyes and place the pieces on the table, floor or anywhere out of reach.
- Fill yourself with a positive emotion – maybe happiness…have a huge smile on your face and sit enjoying your cuppa

When you are ready, burn the pieces or bury them in the garden. You can even shred them. Just be sure to destroy that stopper!

How do you feel? You should feel free!

Write down *why*:

_____
_____
_____
_____
_____
_____
_____

Signature: _____ Date: _____

Letter to my stopper

Dear _____,

_____
_____
_____
_____
_____
_____
_____
_____
_____
_____
_____
_____
_____
_____
_____
_____
_____

I release you with love and light.

Love: _____ Date: _____

Doodles of my fears

Take the time out to think about your fears. Draw them out and depict them in picture form. Discover them and then draw, colour, or paint them! Think of what they mean to you and your life and let the hurt and pain out in your doodles.

Listing my fears

Well done for doodling your fears!

Now you will have a clear picture of what it/they are and how it/they might look to you. Take some time and list the fears that you have and why you might have these fears. Do this in a positive light and with positive emotions, realizing that you are actually facing your fears. What a great thing this is!

Sign and date your list, as this will remind you of when you felt like this. When you revisit your list later, you can see just how far you have come.

Why do I have this fear?

1.

2.

3.

4.

5.

6.

7.

Signature: _____ Date: _____

Replacing my fears

Think about your fears and how they affect your life! Are they real fears or fears that you keep in your mind? Do they keep you behind a wall of fear and dictate the way you live, think, feel, and act?

Be aware that if your fears are real and have to do with a person, people, situation, or if your life is in danger, you must think long and hard about asking for help. Plenty of organizations can and will assist you. Look in your telephone book or on the Internet for contact details. This is very important for your well-being and, of course, your safety.

You have come so far in recognising those fears, some of which can be buried very deep, so now it is time to come up with ideas and strategies on how and what to replace your fears with! Again, just take little steps that will become giant steps as you build upon them.

The fear that holds me back and limits my authentic self is: __

Only you will know what would be a suitable replacer for your fear. Be positive, be realistic, and be brave.

Write out what the replacer is going to be but also fill the whole picture in. Add how you are going to feel, what your emotions and self-talk will be, how you will act …

Write the whole story of what your life will be without this fear.

The replacer that will empower, free me, and build up my authentic self is:

_____
_____
_____
_____
_____
_____
_____
_____
_____

Ideas and strategies on how to replace my fear:

_____
_____
_____
_____
_____
_____
_____
_____
_____
_____
_____
_____
_____

My positive feelings about my replacer:

_____
_____
_____
_____
_____
_____
_____
_____

_____
_____
_____
_____
_____

My positive emotions about my replacer:

_____
_____
_____
_____
_____
_____
_____
_____
_____
_____

My positive self-talk about my replacer:

_____
_____
_____
_____
_____
_____
_____
_____
_____

_____

_____

Remember to sign and date this so when you revisit at a later
stage, you can see how far you have come!

Signature: _____ Date: _____

Time to take a break

Wow, you have worked so very hard and faced some challenging aspects of your life thus far. Well done! It is time for you to take a well-deserved break and do something special for yourself. Not for your children, partner, colleague, neighbour, or anyone … Do something special just for you!

When you are ready, come back to your workbook and carry on but before you do, write down the wonderful thing that you did for yourself in the space below, and if you did more than one thing, good on you, as you are worth it!

Time to take a break

Now that you have had a break write down 'the something special' that you did just for yourself.

My something special was:

14 – Embrace change

Embrace change—instructions

There are two exercises in this chapter of the workbook, for now it is time for you to celebrate and to look at the positives of just how far you have come!

> The real voyage of discovery lies not in seeking new landscapes, but in having new eyes.
> —Marcel Proust[26]

Remember this quote! Read it again and think about how far you have come since starting this book. Even in flicking through it without reading, it would have put a germ of what you can do and how you can do it within your subconscious!

You are seeing through new eyes and becoming aware of what changes and what choices you have if you go out and grab at life.

To celebrate, do this exercise and only write positive points. Leave any negative thoughts, feelings, emotions, self-talk, and actions where they are—in the past.

I have not added lines as before. Why not decorate your page instead? Be creative and celebrate in however you mode you want, but do it with style and with lots of colour, pictures, and sayings. Be proud of it!

Remember to sign and date your tremendous work. Be proud!

---

[26] Refer to chapter 4, "Embrace change"

My changes and choices

These are the changes I have made:

These are the choices I have made:

These are what I feel about them—my thoughts and emotions:

Here is some of my positive self-talk, the words and sentences that I told myself:

Signature: _____ Date: _____

Picture of the new me!

This page is for you to celebrate some more by depicting the *new you*. Do it in any way, shape, or form that you want. This is your page to celebrate in the manner that you want! Think of what you have written on the previous pages and how it is allowing you to blossom and fly free towards finding your authentic self!

Signature: _____ Date: _____

Self-esteem questionnaire

This questionnaire is to enable you to recognise your self-esteem. It is important to realize *how* you view yourself so that you can face and deal with any negative thoughts, feelings, and self-talk. Read the statements below. Think about how they fit into your thinking and then write the number that best relates to you. Remember that self-esteem is the *value* that you place on yourself.

___ I am happy.

___ I love myself.

___ People trust me.

___ Life is enjoyable.

___ I rely on others.

___ My family values my opinions.

___ I attract positive things and people.

___ I look forward to every day.

___ I am kind.

___ I am known for my generosity.

___ I exercise regularly because I am worth it.

__ I have spare time.

__ I can say *no*.

__ I think good thoughts about myself.

__ I believe in myself.

__ I follow my dreams because they are important to me.

__ Wonderful things happen to me because I deserve them.

1	2	3	4	5
Never	Rarely	Occasionally	Mostly	Always

Self-esteem scale

Below is a self-esteem scale for you to do. Think about your answers to the previous exercise and then have another think about the following:

- how your see yourself
- your beliefs, self-talk, feelings, emotions, and actions
- the value that you place upon who and what you are

Once you feel that you have a clear picture of your self-esteem, put a mark on that level on the scale below. I know that this is a hard exercise to do, but it is in this type of reflection that you will realize just how you feel about yourself. Far too often, you can trick your mind and pretend your self-esteem is okay! But if you do not truly realize what is hidden within, how can you ever have a chance to face or change how you feel? How can you ever feel great about yourself, love yourself, follow your dreams, and have positive self-worth?

Low	Medium	High

How did you identify your self-esteem? Was it low, medium, or high? Do not be afraid, upset, or discouraged if your answer was not what you thought it should be or if it was low or medium.[27] This is good news! You can now identify how you feel about yourself and not cover it up. What a great step. It is just one those little steps that you are taking towards that giant step: becoming and knowing your authentic self.

Your journey will consist of many small steps and not one giant one, so step forward in confidence and with courage towards your future.

---

[27] If your self-esteem is at a high level, that is great, and having realized this (if you did not previously), now it is time to consciously work at keeping it high. Negative events, things, and people will certainly have an influence on self-esteem, even if it is high! This is where these types of exercises can help you to keep your positivity!

My thank yous

Many different aspects, events, and people in your life can affect the level of your self-esteem, which implies that the level of it can only be formed by what happens to you. In part, it is—if you let it—but also it is *not*!

There are three aspects to self-esteem:

- It can be due to life itself. Life's events, people, and experiences can dominate and/or shift how you feel about yourself, and if you let them overtake your spirit, they can ultimately influence your thoughts, feelings, and actions—in negative ways.
- It can be a learned skill. By doing self-esteem building activities, the level of yours will lead to a higher level.
- It is an inherent natural gift! Yes, it is there, but it's buried beneath all the stuff that happens in your life. That is why it is so important to create a positive image in your mind of yourself. Create and then believe!

Think what you read earlier about children:

Have you ever noticed how children see things differently—oh so simply? Nothing is complicated and involved, plus they bounce back and forgive so easily. They know what they want and let things go, seemingly without remorse and complications. Why is it that once we reach adulthood, things change?[28]

Yes, children seem to have an endless amount of good self-esteem, confidence, and the ability to bounce back. We are inherently born with that natural gift. But as society, family, rules, and life begin to have an influence, this natural gift is most often buried; the level of self-esteem can, and does, change! Obviously, as we become teenagers, young adults, and beyond, all those influences, experiences, thoughts (whether perceived correctly or not), feelings, and actions make a mark on our personas and can ultimately bury our authentic selves.

It is time to put into place your positive, purposeful thinking and let your self-esteem begin to grow!

From the previous two exercises, you have an idea of the level of your self-esteem, so now it is time to begin to remove your limiting thoughts, feelings, self-talk, and actions! It is time to uncover your natural gift. Put your learning skills into practice and uncover your power!

Once again, sign and date your work, as this is you finding your authentic self!

---

[28] Refer to "Suggestions to my readers on how to use this book," page XV

Look at your life and think about the strengths that have come your way and are in your life, as well as those that will be there in the future. Answer these questions positively!

What have been I good at?

What am I good at?

What will I be good at?

What things have I achieved in my life?

What things am I achieving in my life?

What things will I achieve in my life?

What are my skills, talents, and accomplishments?

What are the challenges that I have overcome?

Signature: _____ Date: _____

Now that you have made a start in recognizing and writing down your positive traits, accomplishments, and how you have overcome in life, keep it up! Below is a blank page for you to ask other positive questions about yourself. When you are ready, answer them. Each day have a look at what you have written and repeat all those positive aspects in your mind. Say them out aloud, reread them, and then take them out into your daily life through your words, feelings, self-talk, and actions!

Practice ... practice ... practice!

My thank yous

My pivotal cue

It is time to start recognizing your self-worth and all the great things that are part of you!

To do this:

- Sit in a quiet place somewhere you are comfortable and still and allow yourself time to reflect and be calm and peaceful.
- Now close your eyes and take yourself back to a time when you felt good about yourself—this should be a positive experience!
- Think about your thoughts, self-talk, feelings, and any actions. Just sit there and *feel* those experiences, soaking them in, and when you are ready, open your eyes and keep that peace, those calm feelings, and those thoughts alive!
- Now write down how you feel—physically, spiritually, and mentally. What are your thoughts, words, and feelings?

My thoughts are:

My words (self-talk) are:

My feelings are:

Physically:

Spiritually:

Mentally:

Signature: _____ Date: _____

Look at what you have written, for this is your pivotal cue—the genuine positive you, the list that you go to in order to read and soak in good things about yourself. Go to it when you are having a bad day, when times seem tough and you can feel the negativity bringing your self-esteem down. This is the list where you remember and feel what it was like at a time when you felt at peace, calm and positive about yourself.

Reading what you have written down will help change your feelings and help you to believe that you have so much worth and deserve to be here ... alive. These words are your pivotal cue to shift your mood and help change your negative feelings into positive ones. Remember to sign and date your work—very important!

Time to take a break from all your hard work and spend some time reflecting and having some *fun*. Time to break out your inner child and be creative by doing some colouring in! Read the words as you colour them in, using what you wish. The idea of this exercise is to reflect on the words and have fun!

Joy

I am happy!

Love

Freedom from pain

Butterflies

I am ME!

Forgiveness

Hope

My dreams

Authenticity

Self esteem Choices changes

I am full of gratefulness for my life

Questions to think about and ask myself

What do I see when I look in the mirror?

What do I think of myself?

Do I know who I really am?

What do I think others think of me?

Signature: _____ Date: _____

What are my negative tapes?

In this exercise, think about your negative tapes. Write down the words and feelings that come to mind—say and feel. In writing them down, you can then begin to acknowledge the negativity and work to change that into positivity.

1.

2.

3.

4.

5.

6.

What are my current burdens?

Look at the previous exercise and what you wrote down. Think about the words and feelings and how they fit into your life.

- Do they enhance your life?
- What do you like/not like about them?
- Have they become burdens that influence some or all parts of your life?

These are hard questions to think about but do so anyway, and when you are ready, answer them. Fit them into the hexagon of your life[29] under the headings below. This will help bring awareness of their place and influence within your life, so use this exercise as a check on where and how negativity is affecting your life.

Remember, by acknowledging any negativity and where it fits into your life, you can then choose to make positive changes.

My negative hexagon of life

Physical:

Spiritual:

Emotional:

Relationships and social:

---

[29]   Refer to "The hexagon of life" on page 15

Leisure:

Environment:

Congratulations on completing this exercise!

Later in the workbook, you will have the chance to look at your hexagon journey, but only from a positive point of view. You can then map it out and fill it with the things that will contribute to working towards a fulfilled and happy life—a step towards your authenticity!

Signature: _____ Date: _____

My list of accumulated negatives for the bin

In truth may you walk and in truth may you live.
Through all the returning seasons may you grow and change,
just as spring turns into summer and summer into autumn and autumn into winter.
May you move and grow with life, singing with the birds, walking through the trails
marked with ferns and trees, with flowers blooming fresh and snow falling thick.
May you live with truth and let truth lead you, guide you,
and help you live your life to the fullest.
You were born in truth. Let you live in truth and finish in truth.

Now it is time to have some *bin fun* as you *biff* your negativities!

Before you start this exercise, find a pen and some paper, a rubbish bag, and your book *Musings of a Blogger*. Now make sure that you have some time, when and where you will have no interruptions, and find a quiet and comfortable spot for you to sit and relax.

- Rip the paper into strips or in half and put the pieces to one side.
- Turn to chapter 16, "What are my current burdens?" and flick to the exercise. Now read what you wrote under each hexagon of life heading. They will be negatives, so you will want to rid yourself of them and think about how they have, or do, affect your life.
- When you are ready, and *only* when, take your pieces of paper and write each negative on a separate piece. Fold it in half and put it in the rubbish bag!

While doing this, this next step is very important. Say aloud in a firm and positive voice, "I release you and let you go!" Remember to say these words for each negative written on the folded paper and put it in the bin.

It is important to not only say these words but also to think them, for the
strength and combination of thoughts, words, and actions is so powerful.

You will realize this anyway as you think of any negative thought, word, and action—whether done by yourself to yourself or if another has done it to you—and these combined are reflected with your life! Are they reflected in a positive way?

Once all those negative aspects are placed in the rubbish bag, tie up the bag and do it with love, grace, and gratitude, as this is a release of the old and the start of the new!

Here is the exciting part—the fun part

Don't you love to biff things? I know that I do, and this is your chance to do so.
Go to your rubbish bin and biff all that negativity … your negativity!
Remember to do it with love, grace, and gratitude, and while you are doing the
biffing, say aloud and think the following: *I release you and let you go!*

Once done, close your eyes, take a deep relaxing breath, and when you are ready, go put the kettle
on. Make a cuppa and sit … relax … and let go!

Now sign and date so that you can revisit when you have biffed your negativities!

Today, the _____ of _____ 20__,

I, _____ _____,

challenged my thought patterns and let my negativity go!

Signature: _____ Date: _____

Positive tapes

Now that you have *binned* your negatives, it has left a space within your life, so it is time to replace that void with positives! So take time to look at your "My positive hexagon of life" below, and as you have thrown out all those negatives into the bin, think of positive things, words, feelings, self-talk, and actions that you want in your life. Take your time and when ready start to write.

My positive hexagon of life

Physical:

Spiritual:

Emotional:

Relationships and Social:

Leisure:

Environment:

Now sign and date this so that you can revisit your positives when you need and want to. In doing this, it also gives you a record of what positive aspects you want in your life as you journey towards learning about and knowing the authentic you!

Today, the _____ of _____ 20___,

I, _____ _____,

will revisit my positive thought patterns to encourage me on my journey to my authentic self.

Signature: _____ Date: _____

My masks

Think of *each* mask that you might wear. Think how it would look if the mask were a physical one and then depict it as a drawing. Colour it, paint it, or decorate it! Include those positive masks as well as any negative ones, but make sure that the masks you depict are those you feel are applicable to you. What kinds of masks are they? Where and when do you wear them? Draw as many or as few masks as you feel are applicable.

My first mask depicts_____.

My first mask is a _____, and I wear it when_____.

Signature: _____ Date: _____

My masks

My second mask depicts _____.

My second mask is a_____, and I wear it when_____.

Signature: _____ Date: _____

My masks

My third mask depicts_____.

My third mask is a _____, and I wear it when_____.

Signature: _____ Date: _____

My masks

My fourth mask depicts_____.

My fourth mask is a _____, and I wear it when_____.

Signature: _____ Date: _____

Why do I wear this/these masks questionnaire

Why do I wear this/these masks? This is a very important question, and you have touched on the answers in the previous exercise, "My Masks," by writing down what your mask is and when you wore it. Have a look back at the answers you wrote and the pictures that depicted your masks in the exercise.

Now take some time to think of your perceptions, beliefs, and feelings associated with your responses before you turn to another exercise, the "My positive tapes—my positive hexagon of life."[30]

Compare the two sets of information—one has a negative slant and the other a positive slant—and think honestly about which set of beliefs about yourself you truly want to be part of your life. Also take time to ponder about who you are and why you think you need any of the masks that you wear. Take some time with this because it is important for you to find answers to these questions.

There are two parts to this questionnaire. Part A is to help you recognise why you wear your masks, and part B is for you to, place your positives instead of your negatives in a particular situation instead.

---

[30]   Refer to chapter 16, "Challenge your thought patterns"

Part A

Peruse the statements in the questionnaire below, and when you feel comfortable, tick the statements that you feel are applicable to you at this moment. These statements are only a small example of why a mask can be worn, so if a statement below is not applicable to you, write one that is in the space provided.

☐ I wear these masks because I feel frightened [all parts of your hexagon of life].

☐ _____

☐ I feel inadequate without my masks when in a social situation [relationships and social].

☐ _____

☐ My physical self is not what I want to be, so I cover it with a mask [physical].

☐ _____

☐ I pretend to be happy where I live, so I wear a "happy" mask [environment].

☐ _____

☐ My relationships are not what I want them to be, so I hide behind a mask [relationships and social].

☐ Spiritually I feel empty and alone [spiritual].

☐ _____

☐ I feel sad all the time, and happiness eludes me, but I laugh and pretend that I am okay [emotional].

☐ _____

☐ I cannot say no, and I hide my feelings of resentment behind an accepting mask [emotional].

☐ _____

☐ I do not exercise or eat in a healthy way because I do not deserve it, but I pretend I do not care [physical and emotional].

☐ _____

☐ I work long hours so that I do not have to face my life, who I am, and do not have time to think, so I hide behind a business mask [leisure, spiritual, and emotional].

☐ _____

Part B

When you are ready, start on part B, but before you do, put those negatives away from your mind and concentrate on all the positives that you wrote in the second exercise, "My positive tapes—my positive hexagon of life."[31]

Think about how you can utilize all those wonderful positive points you wrote down. How can you replace those to cancel out all of your negative beliefs that have formed the masks that you wear?

Part B of this exercise is the place to map this out and start making a plan of cancelling out these negatives and ultimately replacing your masks with your authentic self. This means that you will not have to pretend, cover up, or hide any longer! You can feel a release to be who you were meant to be.

The why, where, and what questions are the feelings, self-talk, beliefs, and actions that all coexist within you and which influence your whole life. If they are negative, they are reflected negatively in all that you do, but if they are positive, your life will be full of positivity.

The statements you ticked previously have been worded slightly differently, but if you wrote your own, this is where you reword it too, to reflect your new positive thinking. Then answer the questions why, where, and what for whichever/some/or *all* the statement(s) that you feel strongly about. Answer them in a positive way from the information written in your "My positive tapes—my positive hexagon of life."

1. I choose not to feel frightened, so upon reflection I ask myself why I do it, where the feelings of fear come from, and what I can say/do to ensure that I am/feel safe [all parts of your hexagon of life].

☐ _____

2. If someone in a social or relationship situation influences me in a negative way, in a way that makes me feel inadequate, I choose to stop these feelings and instead look at the reality of why they do/have done this; where it comes from; and what I can say/do to cancel that negative influence [relationships and social].

☐ _____

---

[31]   Refer to chapter 16, "Challenge your thought patterns"

3. My physical self is not what I want it to be, but do I have a realistic view of myself? I choose to be me, and what I look like is who I am, and I am proud of it, so why do I not feel proud to be me? Where has my dislike of myself come from and what can I do to accept and love myself [physical]?

☐ _____

4. I might not want to live where I do, but I realize that many people live in places far worse than I do, so why am I not happy to be where I am? Where has this feeling come from and what positive things can I do about it? [environment]?

☐ _____

5. Are there really problems within my relationships, and if so, am I with the right people? Do I need to change my friends? Why are these relationships not what I want them to be? Where have they gone wrong, if they really have? What can I say and do for them to be different [relationships and social]?

☐ _____

6. I feel a need to be fulfilled spiritually. Why is this so and where can I go for guidance? What can I do to be happy, contented, and become part of a group [spiritual]?

☐ _____

7. I realize that happiness is waiting there for me and I can easily obtain it, so why do I not feel it? Where can I start to find it, and what will happiness do for me in my life [emotional]?

☐ _____

8. Saying no is not in my vocabulary, and I choose to say, feel, and do only great things, so why am I not saying no? If I choose to say no, where would it be and what do I feel about myself when I say no in situations [emotional]?

☐ _____

9. Exercising and eating well are important for both my physical and emotional health, so why do I not care to exercise or eat in a healthy way? Where can I make good choices and changes, and what will I feel and be like when I do [physical and emotional]?

☐ _____

10. I have plenty of time for myself and enjoy my free time, which is there for the taking, so why do I not reach out and take it? Where can I enjoy spending some downtime? What will it feel like to relax, have fun, and do things for myself [leisure, spiritual, and emotional]?

☐ _____

Now that you have ticked the above statements, or if you wrote your own reworded ones, answer the questions *why*, *where*, and *what*.

Why?

_____
_____
_____
_____
_____
_____
_____
_____
_____
_____
_____
_____
_____
_____
_____
_____
_____
_____
_____
_____
_____
_____
_____
_____
_____
_____
_____
_____
_____

Where?

What?

_____
_____
_____
_____
_____
_____
_____
_____
_____
_____
_____
_____
_____
_____
_____
_____
_____
_____
_____
_____
_____
_____
_____
_____
_____

Sign and date your work too!

Signature: _____ Date: _____

If we are brave enough to face those things that make us
afraid, we can face our fears so much better.
If we are brave enough to face those things that hurt, we can face our hurts with triumph!
Then the fear will not creep into our lives, nor will the hurt overtake.
We will be free to step forwards with courage and find out that we are braver than we think!

Congratulations on coming this far. What challenges you have faced with the exercises in this workbook. Wow! To have done so shows what belief and faith you have in your ability to journey through your life, seeking and achieving happiness as you find your authentic self!

Believe in who you are! Keep your faith strong and your confidence alive, for without belief in your own powers, you will never find the true happiness that you deserve.

Gratitude for the Past and Present

All of us have *good* in our lives—people, events, and happenings—which are found in the day to day and in unplanned and planned experiences, whether a smile, a hug, an unexpected email, time where we can sit and relax, a favourite hobby, a full shopping trolley of food, running water to have a bath, clean clothes … This list can go on and on! Of course, there are also big events that happen in our lives: milestone birthdays, marriages, partnerships, births, new jobs, new houses, and so forth.

Yes, all these aspects of life make up your wonderful moments and, if recognized, will assist in making your life that much better. Even if there are times when you are lonely and things seem challenging it is in recognizing and feeling grateful for even the littlest of things that opens your emotions up to hope. So to start this process of hope, take some time to recognise *all* your good things, however small, and write a huge thank you below. Pick two, three, or more and write them down, then explain why they were good.

1. Thank you for all those good things I have had in the past:

_____

_____

_____

2. Why did I choose to answer the way I did?

_____

_____

_____

_____

_____

_____

_____

_____

_____

_____

_____

_____

_____

3. Thank you for all those good things I have now in the present:

_____

_____

_____

_____

_____

_____

_____

_____

_____

_____

_____

_____

4. Why did I choose to answer the way I did?

_____
_____
_____
_____
_____
_____
_____
_____
_____
_____
_____
_____
_____

Gratitude for the Future

Gratitude is a healing feeling, and with it comes hope, which is why it is such an important emotion. When you experience gratitude, it propels you to a high level on the scale of your emotions. Think about it! When you give thanks[32] or give praise to someone or for something, your body and mind feel brighter. You feel glad and happy—your day seems that much better!

Remember that everything that happens to you has a purpose. It is up to you.
It is your choice to choose how you feel, think, and act upon or about things.
Will you chose to live in negativity or
Will you chose to live in positivity?
Will you chose to say thank you and
Be hopeful, be grateful, or
Will you chose to live in hopelessness and pain?

So does it not stand to reason that if you are lonely or feeling the challenges of life, you should just open your eyes to some of the great things around you? Look at the beauty of the world, the beauty in those little things, and choose to fill your mind, thoughts, self-talk, and feelings with images of all those positive aspects of life! Be grateful for them and give thanks for them; you will discover that your loneliness and despair will change into hope and gladness!

Now that you are feeling hopeful about the present and realize that the past holds many joys, it is also time to give thanks for what is going to happen in your future!

1. Thank you for all those good things I will receive in the future. Name them.

---

[32]   Refer to chapter 15, "Self-esteem—what are your values?" and the exercise "My thank yous." To refresh your memory, have a look at what you wrote there. You may wish to follow through on some of those thank yous here.

_____

_____

_____

_____

_____

2. Why did I choose to answer the way I did?

_____

_____

_____

_____

_____

_____

_____

_____

_____

_____

_____

_____

_____

_____

Look at your *thank yous* often to remind you of hope.
Remember to sign and date them too!

Signature: _____ Date: _____

My Catalogue of Hope

How important gratitude is for cancelling out feelings of loneliness. You can now see how it opens up the way to experiencing hope and in turn a positive frame of mind.

This exercise is for you to write down your own catalogue of hope. It is to inspire you, to encourage you, and to show you how easy it is not to live in loneliness but to reach out and grab life and follow your dreams[33] towards your authentic self!

Have a think about the categories in your hexagon of life.[34] You might want to separate your hopes under each heading. There are six separate spaces for you to do so if you wish.

Write whatever you wish. The world is your oyster so go for it!

1. _____
_____
_____
_____
_____
_____
_____
_____

2. _____
_____
_____
_____
_____
_____
_____

---

[33] Refer to chapter 1, "Do you have a dream?" and chapter 11, "Do you have a dream?" workbook exercises, including "My top three dreams."

[34] Refer to "The hexagon of life" and chapter 17, "The masks that we wear," workbook exercise "Why do I wear this/these masks questionnaire" to refresh your memory.

3. _____

_____

_____

_____

_____

_____

_____

_____

4. _____

_____

_____

_____

_____

_____

_____

_____

5. _____

_____

_____

_____

_____

_____

_____

_____

6. _____

_____

_____

_____

_____

_____

_____

_____

Ordering from my catalogue of hope

Now it is time to have some more fun! Here is where you can order from your catalogue of hope! The more that you have a picture in your mind of what you wish for, the more your feelings, emotions, self-talk, actions, and choices will be positive and hopeful! The more you fill your whole self with happiness, gratitude, and hope, the less you will feel lonely, full of self-doubt and feel wanting!

Gratitude costs nothing. Hope costs nothing. Happiness costs nothing, but loneliness and despair cost you everything!

Name of item	Description	Quantity	Unit price	Tick when ordered
			Free	
			Free	
			Free	
			Free	
			Free	
			Free	
			Free	
			Free	
			Free	
			Free	
			Free	
			Free	
			Free	
			Free	
			Free	
Your order details				
Your complete name				
Your address:				
Your phone number:				

If you require more room, just photocopy your order form and fill it in. Once you have finished your order from "My catalogue of hope," take a photocopy and put it in an envelope. Put your name and address on the back. Write the following address on the front:

To my authentic self
Thank You Avenue
Gratitude
Hope and Happiness 1111

1. Now put a stamp on the envelope and, in your mind, post it in a large bright red letter box. Then physically take your letter and pin it onto your dream wall board.[35] While you do this, give thanks and feel gratitude for all the opportunities that you have, both currently and those you will have in the future.
2. Close your eyes and let any loneliness and sadness go. Instead, feel at peace, free and ready to step further into your journey of life!

Once you have done this, return to your workbook and sign and date that you have sent your order of hope to the universe.

Signature: _____ Date: _____

---

[35] Refer to chapter 11, "My dream wall board" workbook exercise

19 – We can all have happiness—so just go out and grab it!

> If you want to be happy, be.
> —Leo Tolstoy

Yes, happiness is a choice! Whether you really want to face this or not, the reality is that it is your choice. You can choose to be happy or choose to be unhappy!

Remember this motto[36]:
Today is wonderful ... It my choice to celebrate my life and be happy!

Below is your "My happiness scale." Put a mark on the line as to where your happiness lies at this stage in your life. It is important to be honest about this, for awareness of what and how you feel is the key to making changes!

My happiness scale

Low   Medium   High

How did you identify your happiness? Was it low, medium, or high? Again, do not be afraid, upset, or discouraged if your answer was not what you thought it should be or if it was low or medium.[37] Look at this as good news! You can now identify how you feel about your happiness and not cover it up. What a great step. It is just one those little steps that you are taking towards that giant step: becoming and knowing your authentic self.

---

36 Refer to chapter 9, "We can all have happiness—so just go out and grab it!"

37 If you answered high, that is *awesome*! Remember, though, to keep working at being happy because life does at times crowd in. But in saying that, because you have a positive and happy spirit, you will find that when life throws you a lemon, adversity is easier to face! I recommend that you also do the exercises.

My Happiness Questionnaire

Happiness can be many things, and to each of us, it is different because we all *perceive, feel,* and *act* from our own space! So what you perceive, feel, and how you act is who you are. Never judge or measure yourself against anyone else.

This is the same with your level of happiness—what gives and makes you feel happiness is for you alone. Remember these words: What and how you think, feel, and act about yourself and your life is the key to it all! If you seek to be happy by looking at and trying to be just like others, you are not being true to yourself …[38]

Think deeply about how you measured your happiness scale in the previous exercise and reflect on your reasoning as to why you chose the level you did. When you are ready, have a look at the "My happiness questionnaire" and answer the following statements, ticking the ones that are applicable and explaining why. There are ten questions only, but these are a start. Next you will be writing your own sets of statements (all positive) that are applicable to you.

Note: these are all positive statements because in order to bring yourself happiness, you start from a kind and hopeful space within your mind, not a negative space!

1. I choose to look for happiness in everything I do, see, and feel!

☐   Why?

_____

2. I attract positive success and abundance in my life. (Success and abundance does not mean wealth, a high-paying job, and so on. Have a think about what is really meant here.)

☐   Why?

_____

---

[38]   Refer to chapter 9, "We can all have happiness—so just go out and grab it!"

3. I find wonderful things in my life each day!

☐ Why?

_____

4. I can easily feel good about myself.

☐ Why?

_____

5. I attract happiness and abundance because I know I am worth it!

☐ Why?

_____

6. Each day I will find good in at least two things within my life because I know that they are there!

☐ Why?

_____

7. I know that happiness is there waiting there for me. All I have to do is to go out and grab it!

☐ Why?

_____

8. I realize that I have all that I need to be happy, and I am grateful for what life has given and will give to me!

☐ Why?

_____

9. I want to feel happy, and I know that I can!

☐ Why?

_____

10. I am confident in my own life and know that I am happy now!

☐ Why?

_____

You might wonder why these types of questions are included, especially as you might not have ticked many—or maybe none. These questions are here for you to reflect upon and to start you thinking in a more positive way. There are many people who have nothing, yet they are happy. There are many people who have gone through the most terrible adversities, yet they are happy. There are many people who have loved ones who have passed on—children, partners, siblings, parents, and friends—and sometimes in the most dire of circumstances, yet they are happy.

They are happy because they choose to be happy. They choose to let the negative go, and they have decided that life is good!

Now reflect upon this for a moment. Take your time. When you are ready, make up your own positive happiness questionnaire in the space provided below!

Signature: _____ Date: _____

My very own happiness questionnaire

1. _____

☐ Why?

_____

2. _____

☐ Why?

_____

3. _____

☐ Why?

_____

4. _____

☐ Why?

_____

5. _____

☐ Why?

_____

6. _____

☐ Why?

_____

7. _____

☐ Why?

_____

8. _____

☐ Why?

_____

9. _____

☐ Why?

_____

10. _____

☐ Why?

_____

Repeat the following:

I am proud of my happiness questionnaire, and I am going to work every day on being happy!

Take a copy of your happiness questionnaire once you have written your statements and pin it up on your my dream wall board.[39] Look at it daily and be proud of it!

Now sign and date your work.

Signature: _____ Date: _____

---

[39] Refer to chapter 11, "Do you have a dream?" workbook, "My dream wall board."

Doodles of my happiness

Take the time out to think about your happy times. Draw them and depict them in picture form once you discover them. Consider colouring or painting them. Think of what they mean to you and your life and let the good times roll!

20 - Choices, chances, and changes

Wow, you have come such a long way and are nearly at the end of this workbook. This last chapter is very important, as it is an accumulation of all that you have read, learnt, and achieved from working through this book! Before you go any further, have a look back at chapter 10, "Choices, Chances, and Changes," and refresh yourself by reading through the chapter again. Reread the words and rethink the concepts. Perhaps these words ring a bell:

> You must make a choice to take a chance or your life will never change.
> —Michael Baisden

If contrary winds blow strong in your face, go forwards, never turning back. Instead, continue to press forwards, onwards, and upwards, as you do not need to have a lot of might to be victorious! Your life is a journey, a destination, but in the travelling, you have the choice to take the chances, to make those changes that are necessary to live the best life possible for you![40]

Yes, every one of us—and that includes *you*—has choices, chances, and changes within our lives. However, it depends upon the individual—*you*—whether they are recognised and/or even if they are taken.

It depends upon many things, but if you are to be truly happy, choose to make your own journey one of purpose, power, and strength! Choose and take the chance to change what needs changing! No one can do it for you![41]

Take some time to reflect upon chapter 10 before you start the next exercise. It is to help you in your journey of life and to help you balance out your life! Before you start, consider these words:

> And in the end, it's not the years in your life that count. It's the life in your years!
> —Abraham Lincoln

---

[40]   Refer to chapter 10, "Choices, chances, and changes"
[41]   Refer to chapter 10, "Choices, chances, and changes"

My balance sheet towards finding my authentic self!

This balance sheet is to help you towards breaking out from behind that wall—those stoppers, masks, your fear, loneliness, and negativity—and find your authentic self!

Note: This is the final balance sheet within your workbook. When you look back on all the work that you have done in all of the exercises, you will see that you have been balancing aspects of your life without realizing it! Reflect upon this: all these exercises are rather like a balance sheet within accounting. They are allowing you to itemise the facts within your own personal being … and then balance them. If something does not quite add up, then relook at it, work at it, and when ready, rebalance it! You can continue to do this until you feel they are right! This includes all of the aspects that you have looked at:

- dreams
- stoppers
- fear
- change
- self-esteem
- thought patterns
- masks
- loneliness
- hope
- happiness
- choices, chances, and changes

Now it is time to draw up your balance sheet towards your authentic self! Use this sheet to record everything you have done up until today:

- Choose those that you feel have made an impact upon your life.
- Itemize the chances that you have taken.
- Write down the changes that have occurred within your life because of your choices and the chances that you have taken!

Of course, your life has not been all smooth sailing and you have encountered difficulties, facing challenges and adversity, but what about those wonderful things that have happened? All those gems—people, things, and events![42] What about those choices you have made, the chances you

---

[42]   Refer to chapter 15, "Embrace change" exercise in workbook, "My thank yous," and chapter 18, "Loneliness and hope" exercise in workbook, "My catalogue of hope," which is only a smattering of the great things that have been, are, and will be in your life!

have taken, and the changes you have made? Think upon them, as you have made them, and put them on your balance sheet. Become aware of them, which will give you confidence and belief in yourself! These are all those little steps that add up to great steps. They are your balance sheet towards finding your authentic self. Think positive!

My choices, chances, and changes—my accomplishments towards my authentic self!

My balance sheet towards finding my authentic self!	
The choices that I have taken	**The choices that I will take in the future**
Signature:	Date:

The chances that I have taken	The chances that I will take

Signature: Date:

The changes that I have made	The changes that I will make

Signature: Date:

My hexagon journey!

Phew, what a journey you have been on. Well done!

One last thing to do: look back at your exercises before you enter details into the "My hexagon journey." Take a close look at the information you entered in the "My balance sheet towards finding my authentic self" and then think about the concepts within "The hexagon of life." Take your time with this and jot down some notes before you begin. There is some space provided below. Think positive and be positive.

When you are ready, transpose all that positive information, your ideas, dreams, or whatever you want, as this is your record, your inspiration, and your steps towards finding your authentic self!

My preparation notes:

My hexagon journey!

Physical:

Spiritual:

Emotional:

Relationships and social:

Leisure:

Environment:

Congratulations on completing this exercise!

Take a photocopy and then pin it up onto the "My dream wall board" so that you can see all those positive things and how your choices, chances, and changes have made an impact upon your life.

Just one more thing:

Be filled with gratitude and always remember what great potential you have within you! You can do anything that you want to—you have choices and chances and can make as many changes as you want to have a happy life. All those little steps lead to the giant steps that lead you to your authentic self!

Signature: _____ Date: _____

Post-characteristics list

Great things are not done by impulse but by a series of small things brought together.
—Vincent van Gogh

Do these words seem familiar? If you look back at page 37 you will find them there but I have repeated them here, as it is now time for you to take stock of all the work that you have done to get to the end of this workbook. All those seemingly small things you have done throughout this book are only the beginning of your recognising and coming to know your authentic self. I say "seemingly small things" because these steps, the ones that you have taken, those not done by impulse but by choice, all combine to help you achieve greatness within your life! Yes, in taking each small step, you will find the path to your authentic self!

My Post-Characteristics List

Now it is time for you to think about yourself again and make a new list of positive statements about yourself. Do not peek back at your my pre-characteristics list. Instead, write a completely new list. Remember to be positive!

Find all those new things that before you started your journey of discovery were hidden within and buried by self-doubt, negativity, and so forth. As for all those traits that you had never dreamed you had, write them down, look at them, and be proud, for this is just the beginning of your new journey of life!

This time write not five nor ten but fifteen or more positive things about yourself and then tick them with a huge powerful tick. Then laminate your list and put it up somewhere where you can see it every day!

☐ _____

☐ _____

☐ _____

☐ _____

☐ _____

☐ _____

☐ _____

☐ _____

☐ _____

☐ _____

☐ _____

☐ _____

- ☐ _____
- ☐ _____
- ☐ _____
- ☐ _____
- ☐ _____
- ☐ _____
- ☐ _____
- ☐ _____
- ☐ _____
- ☐ _____
- ☐ _____
- ☐ _____
- ☐ _____
- ☐ _____
- ☐ _____
- ☐ _____
- ☐ _____

Photocopy the pages if you need more space. Do not forget to sign and date your entries!

Signature: _____ Date: _____

Now you can have a look at your pre-characteristics list and see just what you wrote back then and what you have written now. Answer the questions below. Write how you feel about what wrote then and what you have written now.

Is there a difference?

If so, what?

What positive aspects have you added?

Can you now identify more great things about yourself than you previously thought you had?

My diploma of authenticity

It is time to recognize your achievements and celebrate the progress and successes that you have had while reading and doing the workbook—so congratulations on reaching the end of this book. To mark the occasion of your journey, follow the instructions below to complete your diploma of authenticity.

Instructions:

- Write your details on the diploma of authenticity.
- Photocopy and frame it.
- Find a place where you can see your diploma each day. It could be on a wall, your desk, in your bedroom, in the kitchen … or wherever suits you. This is extremely important, for in seeing your diploma, you will constantly be reminded of how far you have come and all the work that you have done. Having it in view is one of those positive steps to assist you in your journey of life towards the you that you want to be!
- Each day look at, read, and feel a sense of pride in yourself!

You were born great.
You were born authentic.
You were born with everything you need because you are you.
You are an individual.
You are unique and nobody else can be you.
Believe in yourself and take those steps forwards.
Go out there and make your journey of life your own!

Certificate of Authenticity

This certificate is awarded to:

_____

In recognition of the steps taken
towards achieving authenticity

Signature: _____ Date: _____

Part 3

Reading Group Questions

Reading group questions

If you choose to read this book within your reading group, that is fantastic, but I suggest that you place some ground rules first. This would be especially so if part 4, the reading group questions, are to be discussed within the group. Setting these ground rules allows each participant to feel safe and comfortable whilst conducting this exercise. What you come up with and agree to for your ground rules is of course up to the group as a whole, but I would suggest that you stipulate a privacy and non-disclosure rule at the top of the list. This will open up a line of communication based upon trust, honesty, and love.

a.   a.   There are many themes in this book. Which ones can you identify and relate to?
     b.   How have they influenced your thinking, feelings, self-talk, actions?
     c.   What about your life as a whole?

b.   a.   Name the most important aspect that you learnt whilst reading part 2 of this book.
     b.   How has what you learnt allowed you to make choices, take chances, and make changes in your life?

c.   a.   Thinking back over part 2, what chapter could you identify with the most? Why?
     b.   Has it helped or is it currently helping?

d.   a.   What was the most surprising challenge that you faced while working through the workbook?
     b.   Why was this so?

e.   a.   Regarding the hexagon of life, can you identify with each of the six sides or concepts as a whole?
     b.   How?
     c.   If not, which ones can you not?

f.   a.   Concerning the "Parable of the Butterfly," can you identify with the boy who assisted the butterfly?
     b.   What about the broken butterfly that could not fly?

g.   a.   Do you wear a mask? If so, are you able to let it go?
     b.   Which part and in what way?

h.   a.   Choices, chances, changes! What do you think about these concepts and how do they relate to real life?
     b.   Has what you read in this book influenced you with any of these aspects?
     c.   Are you open to making choices, taking chances, and making some changes in the future?

i.   a.   What did you think of the three aspects of self-esteem that are affected due to life itself—those that can be learned and are natural gifts inherent in all of us?

      b.   Can you relate to these concepts?

      c.   How?

j.   a.   Did chapter 2, concerning the stoppers in our lives, make sense within your life?

      b.   How?

      c.   Do you think it is realistic to rid yourself of these stoppers?

k.   a.   Do you have a dream?

      b.   How did this chapter affect your ideas about those unspoken hidden dreams that you have?

l.   a.   How does the concept of happiness being there for us all if we just go out and grab it sit with you?

m.   a.   Do you think that the concept of "your authentic self" is realistic and attainable?

      b.   If yes, why and how?

      c.   If no, why not?

My wish for my readers is that you all will communicate and share with each other in an atmosphere of love and trust, thereby making, building, and strengthening upon your wonderful friendships.

In life, you do not have to have everything figured out to move towards your authentic self.
The act of moving forwards with a positive step will help
you find the "who" you were meant to be!

My Ideas and Thoughts

Here is some space to think about, brainstorm, and compose your own reading group questions:

My Reading Group Questions:

1.

2.

3.

4.

5.

Part 4

Conclusion

Conclusion

What is life?

What is life? All of us have asked this question at some point in our lives, and we all seek to find the answers—but are there any, and if so, what are they? Many seek the meaning of life through religion, science, or in whatever means they feel will fulfil, or answer, this question.

So what is life? Life is different to each one of us, and the answers we seek can be simple if we only look to ourselves, look inwards, look within.

In life, there is only what you know, not only of the world and how it functions but also the secret life within you.

Our senses and what we see make up our entire beings.

What is life?

It can be found in the daisy hiding in the grass and the swift bird high up above.

Life is the moon shining down upon us from the night-time sky and the fallen snow upon the trees.

It is the sunlit grove where tiny animals hide and the wondrous world where we abide.

> Dear readers,
>
> Go experience life! Experience it in your own way. Live it, taste it, and enjoy it through your own eyes. Remember that each of us is different, with a different path and dream to follow, so live your life to the fullest.

May each of you walk in peace and happiness as you discover, get to know, and live with your *authentic self*!

With love,
Ruth Anne Caukwell
December 2015

Notes

Use the following pages for any notes that you might have when reading the chapters and/or working through the workbook:

Acknowledgements

To my mother, Marie Caukwell, thank you, Mum, for giving me space when I needed it and great support doing the meals, chores, and so much else. Without your love and unfailing belief in me, as well as your physical help and support, my book would still be waiting for the final pages to be written. Love you!

To my sisters, Miriam and Kathleen Caukwell, the 100 per cent belief in my writing and the pride in your voice as you talk about it, plus your love and kindness, has at many times brought me to tears. Thank you, my dears. I am so proud of the women you both are.

To Paul, thank you for the quiet, gentle way in which you encouraged me to take all those little steps on my own—to find and use my inner strength as I journeyed towards finding my authentic self!

I wish to acknowledge those people from Balboa Press who have assisted me in my publishing journey. Their time, expertise, suggestions, and assistance in helping a fledgling author has helped make the experience a delight and so very exciting. Thank you to:

Helen Summers, thank you for your enthusiasm, and support.

Anne Barcelona, thank you for your time, expertise, unfailing assistance, and advice when I asked all those questions and was unsure. Your support made finishing my book hassle-free!

Eric Saxon, Shellie Hurrle and the editing team, thank you for your advice and work on making my manuscript that much better.

To those I have not named, thank you.

Lastly, to all those who have supported me in various ways, including those people who endorsed my raw manuscript, Robert Sheninger, Dr. Robert Minzak, Karen Degen, and Bruce Vesy-Brown, I thank you!

Bibliography

Edwards, R. C. (2008). "Discovering the Body of Butterflies." Garden with Wings—http://www.gardenswithwings.com/facts-info/a0812ButterflyBody.html. Viewed on July 20, 2015.

Tulloch, S. (ed.), *Reader's Digest Oxford Complete Wordfinder: A Unique and Powerful Combination of Dictionary and Thesaurus*, The Reader's Digest Association Limited, Berkeley Square, London, 1993.

Now that you are on the path of finding your authentic self, I suggest reading widely. Read many books that can assist you on your journey! I read constantly, and below are some of the publications I have found tremendously helpful in my continuing journey of life. Some have wise words some have techniques and strategies, and some help me when I feel the negativity coming on. They help me readjust back on the path of positivity.

Once you start, you will find your own repertoire of books, and you might read some from cover to cover and just flick through others. Borrow from the library, which is a great way of deciding whether you want to purchase a certain book. Every day peruse some positive reading material that will fill your soul with *positivity*, which will help carry you through any tougher times!

Byrne, B., *The Secret,* Beyond Words PublishingHillsboro, Oregon, United States, 2006.

Hays, L. L., *You Can Heal Your Life*, Hay House, Inc., California, United States, 1999.

Hays, L. L., *Meditations to Heal Your Life*, Hay House, Inc., California, United States, 2002.

Hays, L. L., *Heart Thoughts: A Treasury of Inner Wisdom,* Hay House, Inc., California, United States, 2012.

Jeffers, S., *Feel the Fear and Do it Anyway*, Vermilion, an imprint of Ebury Publishing (Random House), London, UK, 2007.

Kirwan, J., *All Blacks Don't Cry: A Story of Hope,* Penguin Books, New Zealand, 2010.

Maher S., *Essence: Inspiration for a Life of Abundance and Happiness,* Affirmations Australia Pty Ltd., Bellingen, NSW, Australia, 2008.

McGraw, P. C., *Life Strategies: Stop Making Excuses! Do What Works, Do What Matters,* Vermilion, an imprint of Ebury Publishing (Random House), London, UK, 1999.

Mor, C., *Scratches in the Margin: Wisdom from the Celtic Tradition.* Random House Australia Pty Ltd., Milsons Point, NSW, 1996.

What are your options?
You can step forwards in growth or you can step
backwards into the safety of your old life!

Your journey will consist of many small steps and not one giant one, so step forwards in confidence and with courage towards your future.

About the Author

Ruth Anne Caukwell

Ruth Anne Caukwell is an author, proof reader and editor, inspirational blogger, and teacher.

Born in Christchurch, New Zealand, Ruth's family moved to Tauranga when she was eight, Samoa when she was sixteen, and then Brisbane, Australia, when she was seventeen.

Ruth achieved her first degree, bachelor of modern Asian studies, at Griffith University, Brisbane. She has also received the following diplomas: diploma of freelance journalism, diploma of commercial art, diploma of creative writing, a business diploma, and a proofreading and editing diploma. She is currently studying for a 'Writing for Children' diploma.

Ruth qualified and was accepted into the World Wide Branding Who's Who Registry of Executives, Professionals and Entrepreneurs (for her writing) in July 2015 and was invited to join the Golden Key International Honours Society in 2013.

Ruth had a number of positions during her twenty-year career with the Australian federal government, such as managerial, as a training and coaching coordinator, and as a business analyst for the commissioner of taxation and his executive.

Returning to Christchurch in May 2008, Ruth worked on a contract for Creative New Zealand and as a 2IC at Colorado (while waiting for her university studies to start). Her second degree, a bachelor of teaching and learning—ECE, was achieved in November 2012 before she started teaching in November 2012. Ruth has her full teacher's registration from the Ministry of Education, granted in

December 2014. Ruth went into early childhood education due to a love of children and teaching and to gain an insight into children's art and literature.

Ruth is now concentrating on developing a literary career, as her future goal is to continue her writing, utilizing her literary skills—writing, journalism, proofreading, and editing. She wishes to further her interest in helping women reach their full potential through her inspirational writing. Her other goal is to write and illustrate children's picture books.

Ruth has published two e-books of three short stories each for women about women, which can be found on Amazon: *An Anthology of Three Women: A Mother's Love and Sacrifice for Her Children* and *An Anthology of Three Women 2: Unveiling the True Essence of a Woman.*

Ruth started her inspirational blog in December 2014 and wishes to continue her inspirational writing through this.

Ruth also works as an early childhood teacher part-time.

Ruth's hobbies and interests are playing classical music, art/painting, literature, writing and reading, history, gardening, walking/tramping, and swimming. She loves animals, especially horses, the sea, and being among nature and the natural world.

For more information on Ruth or to contact her, visit:

Inspirational Blog: RuAnCa—http://ruanca.blogspot.co.nz/
Facebook: www.facebook.com/ruthannecaukwell
Twitter: https://twitter.com/ruancaRuth
Email: ruancablogspot@hotmail.com
VIP member Worldwide Branding: http://www.worldwidebranding.com/Ruth%20Anne-Caukwell

Printed in the United States
By Bookmasters